Words by Robin Feiner

A

A is for Arabian.
With a proud head and high tail, the Arabian is one of the oldest horse breeds in the world. Strong, smart, and graceful, it has carried people across deserts for thousands of years.

Bb

B is for **B**elgian Draft.
Big and gentle, the Belgian Draft is strong enough to pull heavy loads on farms. Its kind nature makes it a trusted partner in fields and fairs.

C is for Clydesdale.
With feathered legs and a bold, gentle strength, the Clydesdale is one of the most majestic horses in the world. It moves with proud, steady steps and is often seen in grand parades and countryside celebrations.

Dd

D is for Dutch Warmblood. Elegant and athletic, the Dutch Warmblood shines in the show ring. It leaps and dances with beauty in dressage and jumping events around the world.

E is for Exmoor Pony.
Small but tough, the Exmoor Pony is one of Britain's oldest breeds. It has thick fur and a strong spirit, perfect for life in windy hills and wild moors.

F is for Friesian.
With a shiny black coat and a long, flowing mane, the Friesian looks like it stepped out of a storybook. Once used by knights in armor, today it moves with power and grace in shows and films.

G

Gg

G is for Gypsy Vanner.
The Gypsy Vanner is known for its feathered legs and kind eyes. Bred to pull wagons for traveling families, it's calm, steady, and wonderfully gentle.

H is for Hanoverian.
This athletic horse is a star
in dressage and jumping.
Hanoverians are graceful and
powerful — and often win
medals at the Olympic Games.

I is for Icelandic Horse.
Short and sturdy, the Icelandic Horse can walk, trot, gallop — and even do a special gait called the tölt. It's brave enough to cross snowy mountains and rocky lava fields.

Jj

J is for Jutland.
From the farms of Denmark comes the Jutland, a strong and steady draft horse. Long ago, it pulled wagons, worked fields, and helped build castles.

Kk

K is for Knabstrupper. With its spotty coat like a leopard, the Knabstrupper is easy to spot! This clever and colorful horse is loved for riding, shows, and even circus tricks.

L is for Lipizzaner.
White, elegant, and full of pride, the Lipizzaner performs in the famous Spanish Riding School of Vienna. It can leap high into the air in movements once used in royal courts.

Mm

M is for Morgan.
Strong, friendly, and full of heart — the Morgan is one of America's oldest horse breeds. It can pull a cart, carry a rider, or simply be a loyal friend on the farm.

N is for Nokota.
Once wild on the plains of North Dakota, the Nokota is brave and sure-footed. These horses are part of a proud Native American and frontier story.

Oo

O is for Oldenburg.
Tall and talented, the Oldenburg is built for sport. With smooth movement and a calm mind, it's a favorite in dressage and jumping rings.

P is for Shetland Pony.
Tiny but strong, the Shetland Pony comes from the windy Shetland Islands of Scotland. It's sturdy enough to pull a cart and sweet enough to be a child's best friend.

Qq

Q is for **Q**uarter Horse.
Quick, calm, and clever, the Quarter Horse got its name from being the fastest horse in a quarter-mile race. It's a favorite for cowboys, rodeos, and country trails.

R

R is for Rocky Mountain Horse. With its chocolate coat and silvery mane, the Rocky Mountain Horse looks like a dream. Its smooth, gliding gait makes it perfect for exploring forests and quiet hills.

S is for Standardbred Horse. This speedy horse is a champion in harness racing. Whether trotting or pacing, the Standardbred Horse is known for its strength, stamina, and steady stride.

Tt

T is for Tennessee Walking Horse.
Smooth as silk and gentle to ride,
the Tennessee Walking Horse
moves with a graceful walk
called the ‘running walk.’
It's a favorite for trail rides
and shows.

U is for Ukrainian Riding Horse. Tall and elegant, the Ukrainian Riding Horse was bred for sport and strength. Though rare, it moves with quiet beauty and excels in jumping and dressage.

V is for Vlaamperd.
With a flowing mane and noble walk, the Vlaamperd comes from South Africa. It's a stylish horse that shines in both riding and carriage driving.

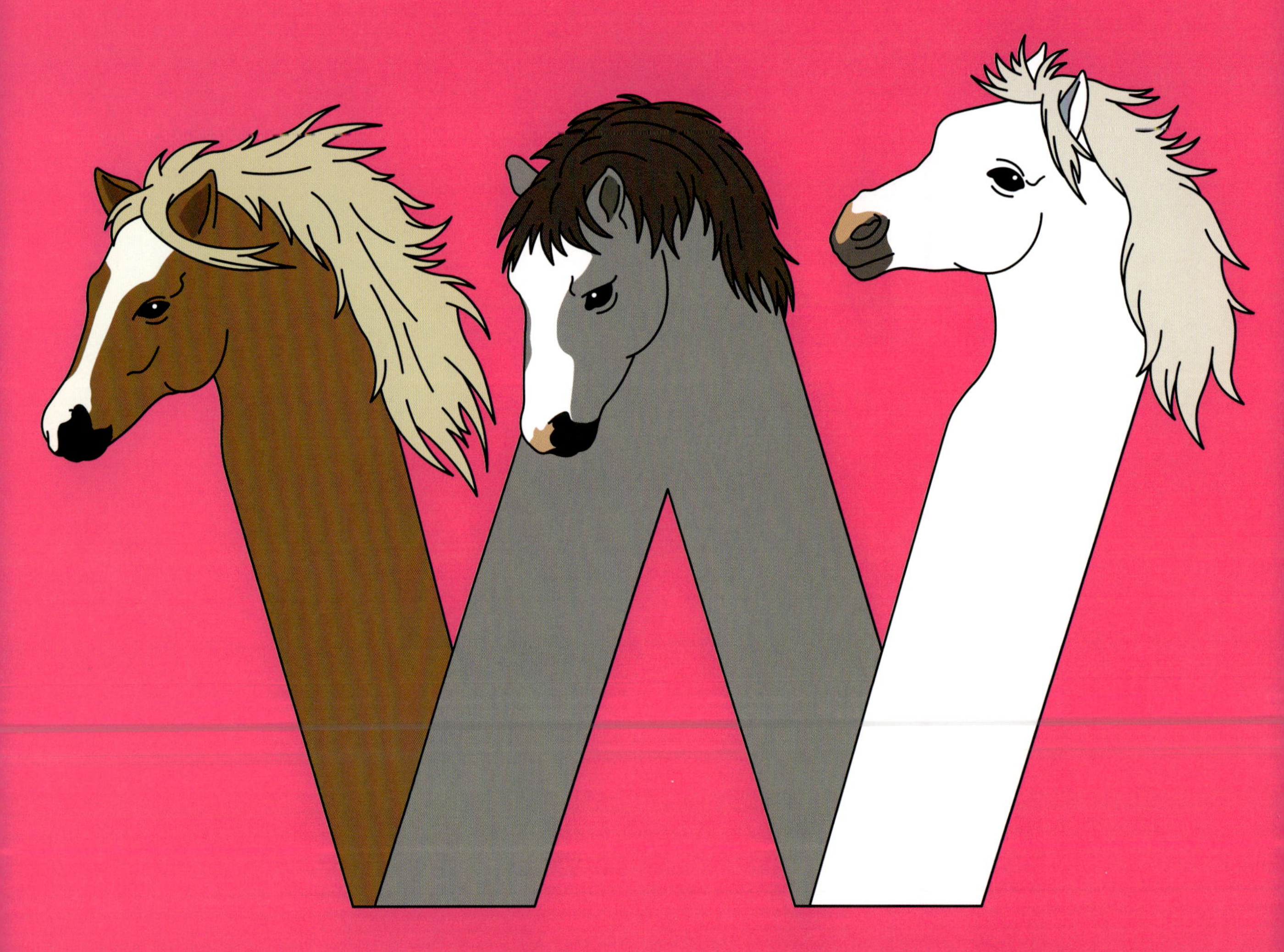

W is for Welsh Pony.
Full of charm and spirit, the Welsh Pony is loved by children all over the world. It may be small, but it can jump, trot, and sparkle in shows and riding lessons.

Xx

X is for Xilingol Horse.
Hardy and hardworking, the Xilingol Horse comes from the grasslands of China. It's strong enough for long journeys and calm living in any weather.

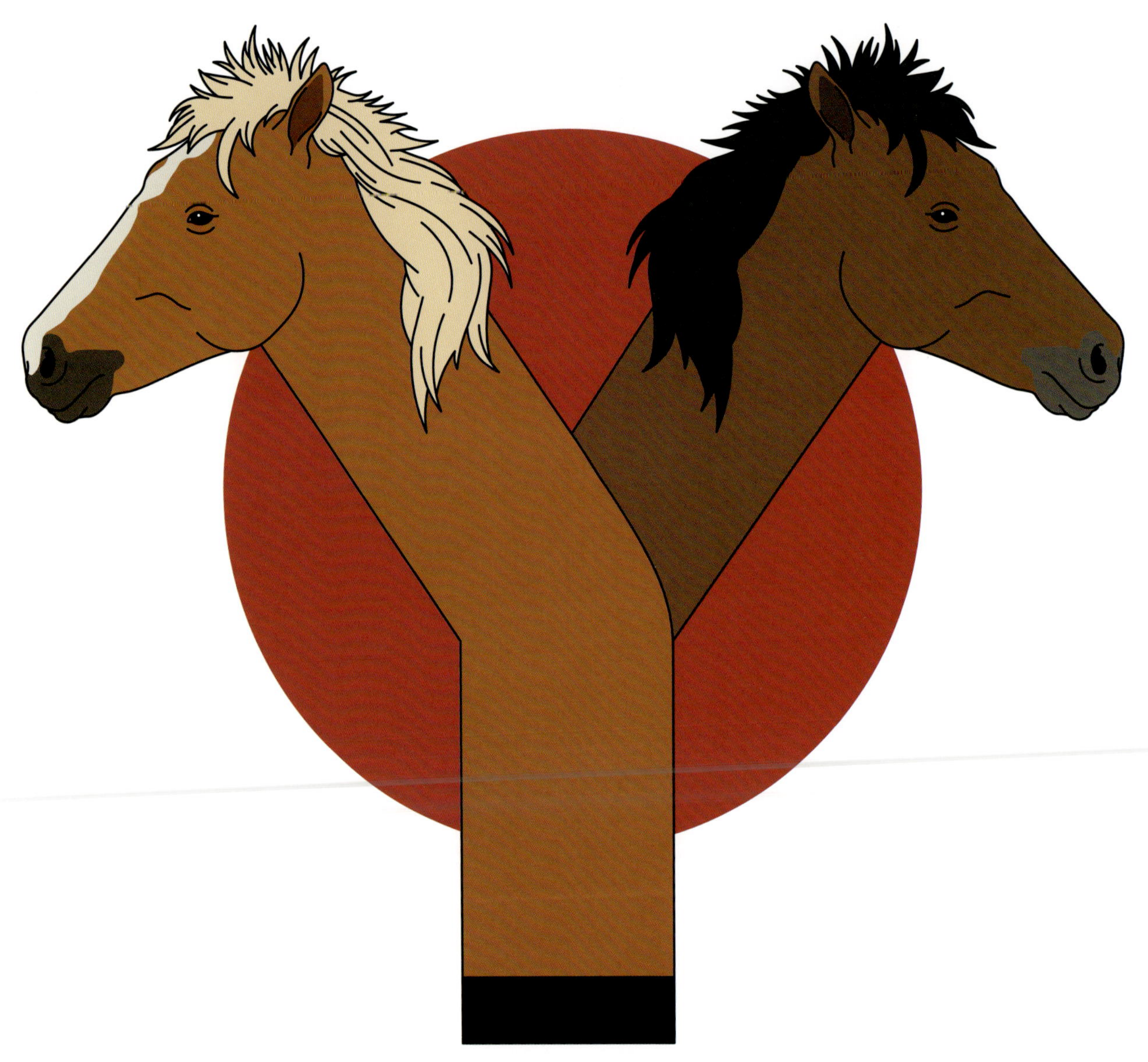

Y is for Yonaguni Horse.
This tiny horse lives on a quiet island in Japan. The Yonaguni Horse is rare and gentle, often seen wandering peacefully near the sea.

Zz

Z is for Zaniskari Horse.
High in the Himalayas lives the Zaniskari Horse, a mountain breed with strong legs and a brave heart. It carries people and packs through snowy trails and steep cliffs.

The ever-expanding legendary library

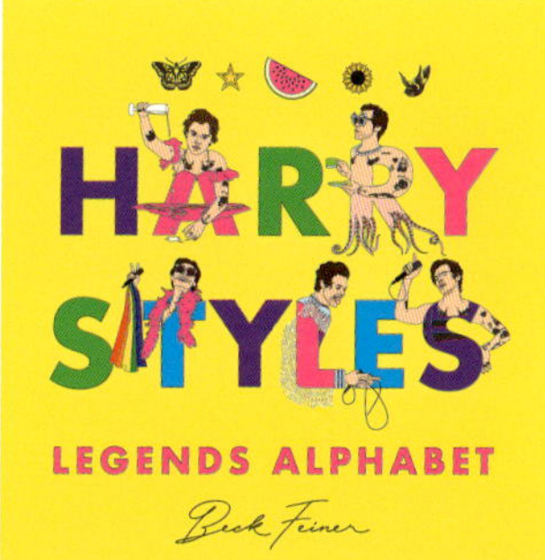

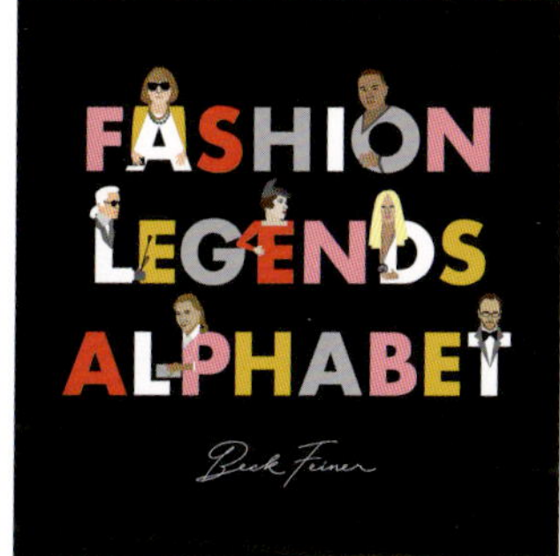

HORSE ALPHABET
www.alphabetlegends.com

Published by Alphabet Legends Pty Ltd in 2025
Created by Beck Feiner

Printed and bound in China.

9781763865242